What others have s

If you think you can read this book unscathed, think again. If your plan is to take a leisurely stroll through its pages, nice try. This in-depth study of the book of Ruth will probe your heart, stretch your mind, and ignite your soul. Expect to be transformed as you enter into a profound and life-changing covenant relationship with the Lord God Almighty through this WOW study of His Word.

—Lisa Elliott
inspirational speaker
and award-winning author of *The Ben Ripple*
and *Dancing in the Rain*

The passion Ruth and Alma have for teaching others about our great covenant with God shows through in every word of this powerful four-part study. The book of Ruth is a beautiful story of love, faithfulness, covenant, and redemption. Working through this study on your own or with a group will give you fresh insight into the sovereignty and grace of God, who is working out His great plan of salvation even in the midst of the chaos and confusion of the times, a moving reminder that He continues to do the same during our own period in history. The imagery of the kinsman-redeemer points ahead to the hope of humanity, Jesus Christ, whose death and resurrection is the ultimate fulfillment of the covenant God made with His people and with all who believe.

—Sara Davison
award-winning author of *The Seven Trilogy*

As Ruth and Alma unpack some of the fundamental truths about God's covenant with us, you will be challenged to take a long look in the mirror of your heart. As we take a longer gaze into the heart of the one making the covenant, we are more able to grasp the depths of Christ's unconditional love and commitment to us and allow our Father to lovingly reveal the areas that still need to be surrendered. This study of Ruth will awaken in you a desire to have the scriptures stitched into the fabric of your heart.

—Rev. Vahen King
Going Farther Ministries
author, speaker, and life coach

Who doesn't love a good story? The book of Ruth—filled with drama, intrigue, and romance—has long been a favourite pick among Bible stories, especially for women. Yet this fresh, compelling study lifts the story to the next level. By skillfully interweaving ancient traditions with modern examples and personal testimony, the story of Ruth becomes our story, too. Whether in personal or group settings, this study is sure to captivate the mind, imagination, and longing heart of readers, illuminating brilliantly our secure place in God's amazing plan of redemption. It is an anointed study, perfectly suited for the changing seasons of every woman's life.

—Keturah Harris
award-winning author of *Reflections from the Waiting Room*

The authors of *Woman of Wisdom* tell the Ruth story, providing information on biblical culture, then giving direction on how to dig deeper and mine for the nuggets of pure gold. *Woman of Wisdom* gives us a place to pause, reflect, and relate to biblical Ruth no matter our culture, age, or what stage we are at in life.

—Joy Presland
life coach

In this Bible study, *Woman of Wisdom*, the authors, Ruth and Alma, reveal the heart of what the Father wanted us to understand about the great exchange we were given through the death and resurrection of Jesus Christ—His righteousness for our sinfulness and His riches for our poverty, just to mention a couple.

The concept of covenant relationship is almost unknown in the North American church, yet God's language all throughout the Bible is covenant language. The book of Ruth so clearly reveals the "hesed" (or "lovingkindness") revealed to this young Moabite woman as she faithfully walks out her covenant with Naomi and with God.

Ruth said, *"Your people will be my people and your God my God"* (Ruth 1:16) In this commitment, Ruth found herself being profoundly blessed by the Lord.

I highly recommend this wisdom study for every pastor and their congregations. How desperately we need to understand the covenant we are to walk in with our God and with one another in the Body of Christ. What a wealth of insight lies within these pages!

—Dr. Gertruda Armaly
Senior Leader/Founder of Antioch Christian Ministries

While reading Ruth Coghill's *Woman of Wisdom* Bible study, I found my heart journeying along a path to our blessed Redeemer. By exploring Old and New Testament covenants, personal stories, and the book of Ruth, WOW weaves a rich tapestry of God's love and provision. This ultimately led me closer and closer to our Saviour, His promises, and a greater awareness of His love. *Woman of Wisdom* is a warm embrace from the Lord from start to finish.

—Cyndi Dejardins Wilkens
international speaker and
author of *Shine On: The Remarkable True Story of a Quadruple Amputee*,
the 2017 Women's Journey of Faith contest winner

*THREADS OF COVENANT
WOVEN THROUGH THE PAGES OF RUTH*

WOMAN of wisdom

A FOUR LESSON BIBLE STUDY

RUTH COGHILL WITH ALMA PETERSEN
FOREWORD BY MARGARET GIBB

WOMAN OF WISDOM
Copyright © 2018 by Ruth Coghill with Alma Petersen

All rights reserved. Neither this publication nor any part of this publication may be reproduced or transmitted in any form or by any means, electronic or mechanical, including photocopying, recording or any information storage and retrieval system, without permission in writing from the author.

All Scripture quotations, unless otherwise indicated, are taken from the Holy Bible, New International Version®, NIV®. Copyright ©1973, 1978, 1984, 2011 by Biblica, Inc.™ Used by permission of Zondervan. All rights reserved worldwide. www.zondervan.com The "NIV" and "New International Version" are trademarks registered in the United States Patent and Trademark Office by Biblica, Inc.™ Scripture quotations marked (NASB) taken from the New American Standard Bible® (NASB), Copyright © 1960, 1962, 1963, 1968, 1971, 1972, 1973, 1975, 1977, 1995 by The Lockman Foundation. Used by permission. www.Lockman.org.

Printed in Canada

ISBN: 978-1-4866-1716-6

Word Alive Press
119 De Baets Street, Winnipeg, MB R2J 3R9
www.wordalivepress.ca

Cataloguing in Publication may be obtained through Library and Archives Canada

Dedication

Woman of Wisdom and the other three Bible studies in the WOW series is dedicated to Mom and Dad, Clara and Bernard Tatton. Their devotion, commitment, and love for God's Word instilled in me a desire for the same. Although our family vessel pitched and rolled on the angry waves of life, my rich spiritual heritage provided an anchor that kept me from drifting too far away. I am forever grateful.

Table of Contents

Foreword   *xi*

Introduction   *xiii*

Lesson One — Determine Your Future

1

Lesson Two — Determine Your Provision

27

Lesson Three — Determine Your Family

49

Lesson Four — Determine Your Eternal Bridegroom

67

Appendix   *93*

Endnotes   *99*

Other books in the WOW series   *103*

Foreword

A young man was about to assume leadership in his nation when God gave him this open invitation: *"Ask for whatever you want me to give you"* (1 Kings 3:5).

The young man, Solomon, was stepping into big shoes. He was following his father, King David, an outstanding strategist and military leader who had lived out his own covenant relationship with God.

Solomon could have asked for many things to ease his responsibility, but he asked for wisdom.

Wisdom: that gift to discern between right and wrong.

Wisdom: that deep heart condition that reveres God and His Word.

Wisdom: that life-empowering and transforming gift that continually draws from the never-ending well of being in a living relationship with God.

Is there a link between wisdom and living in and through a covenant relationship with God? Absolutely!

The story of Ruth and Naomi is an amazing drama of two pitiful widowed women trying to make sense of life after finding themselves again in the rubble of loss. Naomi, the female version of Job, was stripped to nothingness and emptiness. The only thread that held up her life was her relationship with God. That thread became her lifeline to new beginnings when she returned, with her daughter-in-law Ruth, to her roots, her people, and her covenant relationship with God.

Out of covenant came wisdom, and Naomi led Ruth well. Her discernment and soundness of action gave both of them confidence that the God of Israel, their God, would not fail them but would work out His purposes, which would ultimately astonish them and the people of Bethlehem.

Naomi received more than she ever dreamed—a son, Obed. Ruth, a supposed outcast, was listed together with David and Solomon in the genealogy of Jesus.

Ruth Coghill and Alma Petersen, sisters and respected leaders in Canada, have written an incredible study on God's covenant based on the book of Ruth. As you study *Woman of Wisdom*, you will enter into a much greater understanding of God's unchanging, unmoveable commitment to you. What God has established in covenant will empower you, through the Holy Spirit and the power of God's Word, to respond to God's invitation: *"Ask for whatever you want me to give you."*

—Margaret Gibb
Founder & Director
Women Together

Introduction

The brave volunteer from my audience slipped out of the ragged shirt I'd given her to wear earlier, the one covered in permanent black stains, and gave her arms a shake to untangle the tatters hanging around the gaping holes. She looked out over the group of eager participants before shooting a questioning look at me.

Laying the shreds of fabric on the bench, I picked up a beautiful, earth-toned satin cape and placed it around the shoulders that had just shrugged off the rags. Adjusting it at the neckline, and giving the front and back a gentle tug, I fixed the shiny new garment so it hung in neat folds just above her knees. Her eyes grew large and an unmistakable joy slowly surfaced, lighting up her entire face, like a gold-digger spying a gleaming nugget in his mining pan. The impact this moment would have on her life dawned quickly, and everything suddenly seemed different.

The practical application of this simple rags-to-riches exercise emphasizes the exchange of robes so clearly taught in the study of covenant.

It is just one of the many truths that students of this vast topic learn. Those who enter into a covenant with God have the privilege of embracing all the blessings God has provided.

Welcome to the third book in the WOW series, *Woman of Wisdom: Threads of Covenant Woven through the Pages of Ruth*. Our prayer is that you will glean some nuggets as you work through these pages, nuggets that will help you discover how to live in the power, presence, and peace of the One who initiated covenant.

Kay Arthur, founder of Precept Ministries, has written extensively on the topic of covenant. In her book, *Our Covenant God*, Kay writes a summary of the key elements in the ceremony of cutting covenant. We've called it "Covenant: A Brief Overview" and have included it here to provide insights as you begin this study:

Covenant: A Brief Overview

The animals had been slain—cut in half down the spine. Their bright blood stained the stones, the dirt, the grass, vying with sprinklets of wildflowers in their display of color. A covenant was being cut.

The two men stood opposite one another. Each removed his own robes and handed them to the other, then clothed himself in his covenant brother's garment.

I am putting on you... and you me. We are one.

Picking up their weapons from the ground, each handed the other his sword, his bow. By this action they understood...

Your enemies are now mine... and mine yours.

Then they handed each other their belts.

When you are weak, my strength will be there for you.

INTRODUCTION

In a figure-eight path, both walked through the pieces of flesh lying opposite one another. It was a walk into death.

I am dying to my independent living... and to my rights.

They swore by an oath as they pointed first to heaven—

God, do so to me...

and then to the slain animals.

If I break this covenant!

Then each made a cut on his wrist, and with a handclasp the two men mingled their blood.

It is agreed: We—once two—have now become one.

In turn each recited what he owned and what he owed; from this day forward they would share all their resources.

What is mine is yours... what is yours is mine.

Each reached down and scooped up dirt mingled with small stones and rubbed this abrasive into the cut in his wrist.

Wherever I am, when I lift my hand and see the scar, I will remember I have a covenant partner.

They exchanged new names.

Because of covenant I have a new identity.

They sat down to partake of a covenant meal. One broke bread and placed it in his covenant partner's mouth; then the other did the same.

You are eating me, and I you.

Finally a memorial was set up—a pile of stones, a planted tree, a written contract—as a testimony of the covenant they had made.

Now I call you Friend—my friend who sticks closer than a brother.[1]

There are many components in the making of a covenant. It has been said that God speaks the language of covenant, and to understand Him we need an understanding of His covenant language. As we progress through this study, more truths will surface and we will learn more about our covenant-keeping God, our true covenant partner.

We have a lot to learn about God and ourselves in the book of Ruth. If you're ready, let's dig in.

Lesson One

DETERMINE YOUR FUTURE

In a day when common sense rolls off the lips of daytime talk show hosts as though it's a brand-new concept, the need for wisdom is paramount. God's Word is packed with wise nuggets, and its power to guide and direct is highlighted in the life of biblical Ruth.

Although she faced significant challenges, young Ruth refused to let her past dictate her future. God's pleasure in her decision to enter into covenant with Him was displayed in His plan to use her to birth the child Obed, grandfather of King David. Both men were to be ancestors of our Messiah, Jesus Christ.

In this third book of the WOW series, we want to highlight some of the covenant practices which help us to better understand God's plan for mankind. Since we will only scratch the surface of this vast topic, this book's subtitle reads "Threads of Covenant Woven through the Pages of Ruth."

WOMAN OF WISDOM

The Study:

Read the book of Ruth in one sitting. Enjoy the narration and the many emotions that surface throughout. Although only eighty-five verses in length, it is such a significant piece of literature. Try to picture this narrative as a drama.

1. Reread Ruth 1. Jot down a few initial thoughts. When looking for details in a text, it's helpful to answer some of the *w* and *h* questions: *who, what, when, where, why,* and *how*?

   Naomi has lost her husband and two sons, is bitter. Ruth is loyal to her mother-in-law Naomi.

2. When does the story take place, according to Ruth 1:1? What was the behaviour of man like during the time of the judges? The following scripture will give you biblical insight.

Judges 17:6, NASB

In those days there was no king in Israel; every man did what was right in his own eyes.

The story takes place in the days when the judges ruled. People were living for themselves.

LESSON ONE - DETERMINE YOUR FUTURE

3. What would life be like if everyone did what was right in their own eyes? Can you name specifics from today's culture where you see this trend escalating?

It wouldn't be very nice. Divorce, common-law marriage, addictions, no prayer in schools, abortion, gender issues, violence, crime.

4. Who are the main characters in Ruth 1? In biblical times, a person's name suggested his or her character, which can be seen lived out in their individual stories. If you can find the meaning of each of their names online, or in a Bible dictionary, write them out here.

Naomi (pleasant) - Mara (bitter) / Ruth (friend, beauty) Boaz (strength, quickness)

5. a) What are the geographical locations mentioned in Ruth 1? Write one or two details about each place and its significance to God's people.

Bethlehem - fertile, city of David, birthplace of Christ,

WOMAN OF WISDOM

Moab - now Jordan

The story begins in Bethlehem, which means "house of bread," the place of the Messiah's birth. Later in the New Testament, Jesus reveals a significant truth to God's people. Discuss the following verse in light of Bethlehem.

JOHN 6:35, 41
Then Jesus declared, "I am the bread of life. Whoever comes to me will never go hungry, and whoever believes in me will never be thirsty... I am the bread that came down from heaven."

bread was a staple, provides nourishment and comfort. The word (Bible) is bread for our soul, helps us know how to follow God.

b) Why does Elimelech move his family to Moab? According to Deuteronomy 23:3–6, was Moab a good location to settle his family?

DEUTERONOMY 23:3–6
No Ammonite or Moabite or any of their descendants may enter the assembly of the Lord, not even in the

LESSON ONE - DETERMINE YOUR FUTURE

tenth generation. For they did not come to meet you with bread and water on your way when you came out of Egypt, and they hired Balaam son of Beor from Pethor in Aram Naharaim to pronounce a curse on you. However, the Lord your God would not listen to Balaam — *false prophet* but turned the curse into a blessing for you, because the Lord your God loves you. Do not seek a treaty of friendship with them as long as you live.

Elimelech moved his family to Moab because there was a famine. It wasn't a particularly good location to settle Elimelech's family

Scripture records many reasons for not associating with the Moabites. If you want to discover more about Moab's origins and God's instruction to His people in dealing with the Moabites, read Genesis 19:30–38 and Numbers 22–25.[2] Add your insights on the lines below.

The Moabites came from incest.

6. a) What are the two reasons Moses gives in Deuteronomy 23:4 for not permitting the sons of Israel to associate with the Moabites?

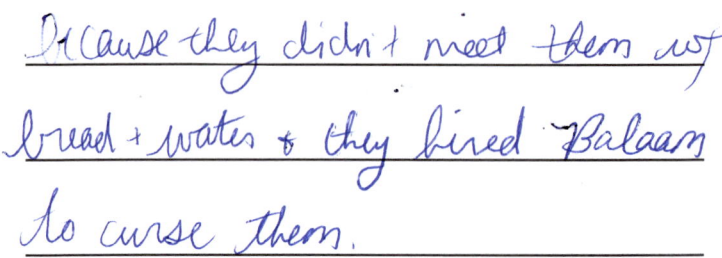

Because they didn't meet them w/ bread + water & they hired Balaam to curse them.

The first reason doesn't concern their idols or their origin, but rather refers to the fact that the Moabites didn't provide needed food and water when the sons of Israel passed through Moab on their way out of Egypt. The Moabites refused to offer hospitality.

Entertaining others in our homes is a gift that we often neglect. I've wondered if, in an effort to have a perfect meal or a spotless house, I have missed opportunities to entertain angels, those who are in need of not only home-cooked fare but also the warmth and love that come from fellowship around a table. Is it necessary to serve steak and baked potatoes to open the door to encouraging others?

Several years ago, our family provided music for a church on the other side of our town. As guests, we were invited to the pastor's house for lunch following the morning service. As we entered the lovely, modern home, I didn't smell a roast cooking, nor did I see any evidence of food or table preparation for our visit. The pastor, his wife, and all of us settled in the comfy chairs in the living room. I wondered if they were hungry too.

Soon the pastor's wife stood and walked to the kitchen in full view. She took some cans out of the cupboard and invited me to help open the tuna and add the ingredients for sandwiches. She opened the dill pickles, placed carrots and celery on a tray, and then put on the tea.

Hospitality took on a deeper meaning that day. This experience gave me confidence to realize that peanut butter and jam can be a feast

LESSON ONE - DETERMINE YOUR FUTURE

when shared with those who dare to keep hospitality simple in the midst of a hectic life.

    b) What do the following scriptures suggest about the importance God places on caring for others, even strangers?

ROMANS 12:13
Share with the Lord's people who are in need. Practice hospitality.

1 TIMOTHY 5:10
...and is well known for her good deeds, such as bringing up children, showing hospitality, washing the feet of the Lord's people, helping those in trouble and devoting herself to all kinds of good deeds.

1 PETER 4:9
Offer hospitality to one another without grumbling.

Caring for others is a good thing to do - without complaining

If you have the gift of entertaining and make guests or strangers feel at home, don't underestimate its value. Hospitality is woven into the fabric of covenant. After vows were made and sacrifices offered, the participants cutting the covenant sat down to enjoy a delicious meal, a

WOMAN OF WISDOM

[handwritten: ended on March 10th]

celebration of the occasion. (See Kay Arthur's summary in the Introduction: Covenant-A Brief Overview)

In question 2, you discovered that the story takes place in the days *"when the judges ruled"* (Ruth 1:1). To put that in perspective, note that the book of Ruth takes place long after Moses died. Joshua was the next leader, and he helped Israel conquer and settle the Promised Land. After Joshua's death, there was a period of about three hundred years when God raised up judges to rule the people. Scholars believe the story of Ruth took place around the time of the famine during Gideon's life, recorded in Judges 6.

Since we're looking at threads of covenant in this book, we need to go back to the time of Moses and review the covenant that God established with His chosen people. Known as the Old Covenant, found in the book of Exodus, it was passed down orally to each successive generation. The following scriptures would have been very familiar to Elimelech's family.

Exodus 19:1–8

On the first day of the third month after the Israelites left Egypt—on that very day—they came to the Desert of Sinai. After they set out from Rephidim, they entered the Desert of Sinai, and Israel camped there in the desert in front of the mountain.

Then Moses went up to God, and the Lord called to him from the mountain and said, "This is what you are to say to the descendants of Jacob and what you are to tell the people of Israel: 'You yourselves have seen what I did to Egypt, and how I carried you on eagles' wings and brought you to myself. Now if you obey me fully and keep my covenant, then out of all nations you will be my treasured possession. Although the whole earth is mine, you will be for me a kingdom of priests and a holy nation.' These are the words you are to speak to the Israelites."

So Moses went back and summoned the elders of the people and set before them all the words the Lord had commanded him to speak. The people all responded together, "We will do everything the Lord has said." So Moses brought their answer back to the Lord.

Exodus 24:3–8

When Moses went and told the people all the Lord's words and laws, they responded with one voice, "Everything the Lord has said we will do." Moses then wrote down everything the Lord had said.

He got up early the next morning and built an altar at the foot of the mountain and set up twelve stone pillars representing the twelve tribes of Israel. Then he sent young Israelite men, and they offered burnt offerings and sacrificed young bulls as fellowship offerings to the Lord. Moses took half of the blood and put it in bowls, and the other half he splashed against the altar. Then he took the Book of the Covenant and read it to the people. They responded, "We will do everything the Lord has said; we will obey."

Moses then took the blood, sprinkled it on the people and said, "This is the blood of the covenant that the Lord has made with you in accordance with all these words."

Did you notice that Moses collected the blood in two bowls? To refresh your memory on the significance of his actions, review the introduction at the front of this study and read Kay Arthur's words in Covenant: A Brief Overview.

WOMAN OF WISDOM

7. a) Who initiated the covenant?

    ?

    b) What did God desire from His people as their part of the covenant relationship?

    that they would do everything he said.

    c) How did the people respond?

    they said they'd do everything God said.

    d) What was the sign that a covenant had taken place?

    blood sprinkling

LESSON ONE - DETERMINE YOUR FUTURE

    e)   Here are the terms of the covenant. How would you describe them?

Up to here for March 10th.

Exodus 20:1–17

And God spoke all these words:

"I am the Lord your God, who brought you out of Egypt, out of the land of slavery.

"You shall have no other gods before me.

"You shall not make for yourself an image in the form of anything in heaven above or on the earth beneath or in the waters below. You shall not bow down to them or worship them; for I, the Lord your God, am a jealous God, punishing the children for the sin of the parents to the third and fourth generation of those who hate me, but showing love to a thousand generations of those who love me and keep my commandments.

"You shall not misuse the name of the Lord your God, for the Lord will not hold anyone guiltless who misuses his name.

"Remember the Sabbath day by keeping it holy. Six days you shall labor and do all your work, but the seventh day is a sabbath to the Lord your God. On it you shall not do any work, neither you, nor your son or daughter, nor your male or female servant, nor your animals, nor any foreigner residing in your towns. For in six days the Lord made the heavens and the earth, the sea, and all that is in them, but he rested on the seventh day. Therefore the Lord blessed the Sabbath day and made it holy.

"Honor your father and your mother, so that you may live long in the land the Lord your God is giving you.

"You shall not murder.

"You shall not commit adultery.

"You shall not steal.

"You shall not give false testimony against your neighbor.

"You shall not covet your neighbor's house. You shall not covet your neighbor's wife, or his male or female servant, his ox or donkey, or anything that belongs to your neighbor."

Comprehensive.

_____

_____

8. a) Read the following verses. List the blessings that God promises His people for their obedience.

DEUTERONOMY 7:9–14

Know therefore that the Lord your God is God; he is the faithful God, keeping his covenant of love to a thousand generations of those who love him and keep his commandments. But those who hate him he will repay to their face by destruction; he will not be slow to repay

LESSON ONE - DETERMINE YOUR FUTURE

to their face those who hate him. Therefore, take care to follow the commands, decrees and laws I give you today.

If you pay attention to these laws and are careful to follow them, then the Lord your God will keep his covenant of love with you, as he swore to your ancestors. He will love you and bless you and increase your numbers. He will bless the fruit of your womb, the crops of your land—your grain, new wine and olive oil—the calves of your herds and the lambs of your flocks in the land he swore to your ancestors to give you. You will be blessed more than any other people; none of your men or women will be childless, nor will any of your livestock be without young.

_____

_____

_____

b) Read Deuteronomy 11:13–17. Why might God's chosen people be experiencing a famine?

[handwritten response]

DEUTERONOMY 11:13–17
So if you faithfully obey the commands I am giving you today—to love the Lord your God and to serve him with all your heart and with all your soul—then I will send rain on your land in its season, both autumn and spring rains, so that you may gather in your grain, new

wine and olive oil. I will provide grass in the fields for your cattle, and you will eat and be satisfied.

Be careful, or you will be enticed to turn away and worship other gods and bow down to them. Then the Lord's anger will burn against you, and he will shut up the heavens so that it will not rain and the ground will yield no produce, and you will soon perish from the good land the Lord is giving you.

_____

_____

_____

c) What kind of judgments would God bring upon them?

_____

_____

_____

All of this took place under the Old Covenant. God is a God of love and also a God of covenant. When we enter into a covenant with God, there are things we can expect from Him and things He requires from us. The Ten Commandments were also included in God's instructions, but the people refused to repent and return to Him when they found the laws impossible to keep.

LESSON ONE - DETERMINE YOUR FUTURE

Thankfully, a New Covenant was promised, fulfilled by Jesus, the Messiah. This New Covenant is written on our hearts. Hallelujah! What a promise! What a Saviour![3]

9. What happened to Elimelech's family, according to Ruth 1:3–5?

They all died (her two sons and her husband)

10. Why did Naomi decide to return to Bethlehem in Ruth 1:6?

for grain (food) and to be with family.

Sinclair Ferguson, in his book *Faithful God*, expresses a deeper meaning to the word *return*, which is used over and over again in Ruth 1:

> The constant repetition of this particular verb is significant because it is not only the Hebrew word for "return," but it is the Old Testament's word for turning back to God's covenant grace and mercy—for repentance, for conversion.[4]

for March 17th

WOMAN OF WISDOM

Remember as a child when your mother repeatedly said, "Be home before dark"? The next day you would hear it again: "Be home before dark." Repetition is often used for emphasis, and certainly when the Hebrew people heard the word *return* over and over again, they got the idea that it was time to go back where they belonged.

Naomi needed to go back to Bethlehem, the house of bread, for that was the only place she would find nourishment, not only for her body but also for her soul.

> ## MATTHEW 4:4
> Jesus answered, "It is written: 'Man does not live on bread alone, but on every word that comes from the mouth of God.'"

11. In the chart below, compare the responses of Ruth and Orpah to Naomi's request that they return to Moab.

	ORPAH	RUTH
Emotional Response	cried	cried
Physical Response	kissed Naomi goodbye	
The Choice	returned to Moab, her people and her gods	
Result		

LESSON ONE - DETERMINE YOUR FUTURE

DEUTERONOMY 30:19
This day I call the heavens and the earth as witnesses against you that I have set before you life and death, blessings and curses. Now choose life, so that you and your children may live...

Orpah returned to Moab, her people, and her gods. That was her choice, and from a human perspective it was a logical one. However, we never hear of her again.

Moab could represent the god we choose instead of returning to the one true God. Some of us have chosen the god of success, the god of popularity, the god of food, or the god of drugs and alcohol to bring us satisfaction. But returning to the one true God is the only way to find lasting satisfaction.

Bethlehem, centuries later, became the birthplace of Jesus, the Bread of Life.

12. Read Ruth 1:16–17. What does this declaration tell you about Ruth?

   She is very committed and determined.

At the beginning of Ruth 1, we see a thread of covenant. Ruth made a vow, not only to Naomi but also to Naomi's God. Since we know the end of the story, we also know that she kept this promise and fulfilled her covenant responsibility. Vows are an essential element of covenant.

Naomi was part of the Old Covenant, made with the sons of Israel at the time of Moses. She understood the covenant words that Ruth used in making her promise.

In Genesis 15, long before Moses and the establishment of the Old Covenant, we read that God set up the pattern for covenant-making with Abraham, a pattern practiced by cultures and tribes ever since.[5]

RUTH 1:18–19
When Naomi realized that Ruth was determined to go with her, she stopped urging her.

So the two women went on until they came to Bethlehem. When they arrived in Bethlehem, the whole town was stirred because of them, and the women exclaimed, "Can this be Naomi?"

13. How would the two women get back to Bethlehem? What challenges might they have faced on their journey?

14. Contrast the different realities Ruth and Naomi experienced when they arrived in Bethlehem.

LESSON ONE - DETERMINE YOUR FUTURE

NAOMI	RUTH

15. a) Why did the women exclaim, *"Can this be Naomi?"*

_____

_____

_____

b) Why did Naomi blame God for her current situation? See Ruth 1:20–21.

_____

_____

_____

c) What are your thoughts about God in your present circumstances?

_____

16. Record the different names that Naomi attributes to God in Ruth 1.

_____

_____

_____

17. What is significant about the time (season) of their arrival in Bethlehem? See Ruth 1:22.

_____

_____

_____

It was the season for Naomi to return, for she belonged in Bethlehem, the house of bread. Ruth also belonged in Bethlehem, not by birth, but because of her covenant pledge to Naomi's God.

What a beautiful picture this story emphasizes. God has provided a way for the foreigner, the Gentiles, you and me, to enter into the everlasting covenant. And what a reminder that our future destiny is not a

LESSON ONE - DETERMINE YOUR FUTURE

matter of chance, but a matter of our choice to follow God all the way to Christ, our Messiah!

The women arrived safely in Bethlehem, the place where not only would their stomachs be filled, but their longings satisfied and their spirits nourished.

18. What have you learned about God and His activity in people's lives from Ruth 1?

_____

_____

_____

19. How will you apply what you have learned this week? Be specific.

_____

_____

_____

You have just completed the study segment of Lesson One. There are three more segments—the summary statement,[6] the memory verses,[7] and the story. Stay with us to the end. You'll be glad that you did.

We pray that you will take time in the coming days to be still and meditate on all that the Spirit has shown you. This will greatly enhance your adventure.

WOMAN OF WISDOM

Lesson One Summary Statement
"Entering into God's covenant determines your future."

MEMORY VERSE:

RUTH 1:16–17

But Ruth replied, "Don't urge me to leave you or to turn back from you. Where you go I will go, and where you stay I will stay. Your people will be my people and your God my God. Where you die I will die, and there I will be buried. May the Lord deal with me, be it ever so severely, if even death separates you and me."

Write out the verses on the lines provided.

_____

_____

_____

_____

_____

LESSON ONE - DETERMINE YOUR FUTURE

Notes

WOMAN OF WISDOM

Notes

LESSON ONE - DETERMINE YOUR FUTURE

The Story: Alma, Part One

I don't need God in my life, I thought. *I am strong. I can handle anything that comes my way. I am in control.*

At sixteen, I decided that belief in God was only for weak, dependent people who needed a crutch. Perhaps my decision was strongly influenced by observing my father, who was a dynamic believer in Jesus but who also suffered from mental illness.

I fell in love with a man who called me Princess and treated me like one. I married him, totally convinced that my life would have a fairy-tale ending. He had a similar upbringing to mine and had also decided that he didn't need God in his life. Those early years of marriage seemed perfect to me. I was doing very well without God. I was in control.

There were, however, things that troubled me, events over which I had no control. The Cold War between Russia and the United States was at its peak when I began my teaching career in the early 1960s. I distinctly remember the chilling sound of air raid sirens being tested in our Toronto neighbourhood. As teachers, we had a great responsibility: the safety of our children.

Frequently we practiced the drill to be used in the event of an attack on our city. When the alarm sounded, I quickly instructed my Grade One class to line up and walk to the basement. There, the children would sit on the floor, backs to the wall and heads between their knees, awaiting the bomb.

The principal suggested the possibility of another evacuation plan if time permitted, at least half an hour. In this scenario, I would take my students to their homes. I kept a copy of the designated route in my desk drawer.

"And what about the teachers?" I asked him. "Where will they take shelter?"

"Well," he replied, "by the time all the children are delivered, the thirty minutes will be up. You're on your own."

Alone? On an empty street? No escape and no place to go? I was not in control.

And then there was the day that John F. Kennedy was assassinated. My heart pounded when I heard the news. Anxiety was evident in the restless behaviour of my thirty-two little Grade One children that day.

Will they hear my heart thumping? I wondered. *How can I keep them calm?*

I gathered them around me, picked up a Bible storybook, and read to them. As I finished, a hush settled over us—an unexplained, supernatural peace.

Not long after, I began to observe a genuine Christian couple. I saw love, joy, and peace in their lives. Their quiet confidence in the midst of unnerving circumstances proved to me that my carefully controlled world, without God, did not have all the answers. I longed to be like them. I sensed God's love reaching out to me. I yearned to respond to that love.

One day, months later, my yearning heart could take it no longer. I left school at noon and walked to my apartment. I fell down on my knees in front of our sofa.

"God," I prayed, "I've shut you out of my life for twenty-six years. I don't know anything about you. But if you are really there, come in and take control of my life and be my teacher."

That day began my covenant relationship with God. My life is forever changed.

Lesson Two

DETERMINE YOUR PROVISION

Defining moments. All of us have them—sickness, financial crisis, the loss of a mate through death, betrayal or divorce, loss of a job, a move away from family and friends, and other life-altering circumstances. In Ruth 1, Naomi and Ruth had many such moments, leaving them broken, vulnerable, and without provision.

How we respond to life's changes and challenges will make a difference in the impact we have in God's kingdom. Ruth and Naomi demonstrate to us how to live wisely in spite of any situation.

We don't want you to miss a single truth God has for you in Lesson Two, which continues this timeless story and covers the second chapter of Ruth.

Before starting, pause and ask the Holy Spirit to open your eyes to the truths you need to see today. God makes it clear that we can know Him, but knowing Him comes with a specific requirement. We find the answer in Psalm 46:10: *"Be still, and know that I am God."*

The Study:

1. Read Ruth 2. Jot down your initial thoughts.

   _____

   _____

   _____

2. How is Ruth's covenant promise to Naomi, as recorded in Ruth 1:16–17, impacting her life in Ruth 2?

   _____

   _____

   _____

With God as her witness—*"May the Lord deal with me, be it ever so severely, if even death separates you and me"* (Ruth 1:17)—Ruth boldly made a life-changing choice. Because she decided to follow the God of Abraham, Isaac, and Jacob, she received all of His blessings.

One of the most freeing principles possible for us today is to live in light of God's covenant with us. It enables us to be the women of wisdom He calls us to be. There is no fence-sitting, though. Each of us makes a choice to forget the past and move out of our comfort zone. We can run *to* or *from* God because of our circumstances. One thing is for certain: entering into covenant with our God will always make a difference in our lives.

LESSON TWO - DETERMINE YOUR PROVISION

3. What does the phrase *"pick up the leftover grain"* in Ruth 2:2 indicate about Ruth's status in Bethlehem? Write what you discover about God's provision on the lines provided below.

LEVITICUS 23:22, NASB

When you reap the harvest of your land, moreover, you shall not reap to the very corners of your field nor gather the gleaning of your harvest; you are to leave them for the needy and the alien. I am the Lord your God.

DEUTERONOMY 24:19, NASB

When you reap your harvest in your field and have forgotten a sheaf in the field, you shall not go back to get it; it shall be for the alien, for the orphan, and for the widow, in order that the Lord your God may bless you in all the work of your hands.

_____

_____

_____

Arnold Fruchtenbaum, in his book *The Books of Judges and Ruth*, writes:

> Hostile landowners, unbelieving landowners, would have ways of making gleaning difficult for the poor. So for that reason, it was better to look for someone who was friendly toward the poor. Furthermore Ruth may

not have actually known the laws of her newly adopted country. All of this will set the stage for the attitude of Boaz toward a foreigner like her. The extreme poverty that forced Ruth to pick the fields like any pauper was no coincidence, but it was a foreshadowing of that poor man, riding a donkey (Zec. 9:9) that would descend from her—(He would be) the Messiah.[8]

God loves to provide for His own. It is His nature to give good gifts to His children. In Ruth 1:6, Scripture records that Naomi heard that the Lord had come to the aid of His people by providing food for them. Let's never forget that one of God's names is Jehovah-Jireh, God the Provider. It's His promise in Genesis 22. God has faithfully made provision for the poor and needy; man has not always had the compassionate heart of God.

The stage is now set for Boaz, a man who exudes God's lovingkindness and compassion. Through Boaz, God shows a more perfect way to demonstrate His provision.

> 4. Underline each of the characters' names in the text: Naomi, Ruth, and Boaz. List what you learn about each of them.

_____

_____

_____

Let's read what Arnold G. Fruchtenbaum writes about Boaz:

LESSON TWO - DETERMINE YOUR PROVISION

By Rabbinic tradition, Boaz was about eighty years old when he married Ruth, and was a childless widower. As to his status, the text states that Boaz was: a mighty man of wealth, a translation of two Hebrew words. The first Hebrew word is gibbor, which means "a mighty man of valor", and conveys the concept of one who was capable, efficient, worthy in battle, and exceptionally important or powerful in a specific field. The most common usage of this term connotes military activity, military service, someone who is able to bear arms, or one who has already distinguished himself by performing heroic deeds. It is also used prophetically of the Messiah in Isaiah 9:6. The second Hebrew word is chayil, which means "strength". It is generally used of a warrior in a military sense. The terms emphasize Boaz was a man of distinction, a man of wealth. Here chayil is not used in the military sense, but in the sense of a wealthy landowner. Boaz was an efficient, capable, and wealthy landowner in his community, and one who lived an exemplary lifestyle. This same term is used of Ruth in 3:11.[9]

5. According to Matthew 1:5, who are the parents of Boaz? How might his heritage have influenced his generosity towards Ruth?

MATTHEW 1:5
Salmon was the father of Boaz by Rahab, Boaz was the father of Obed by Ruth, and Obed the father of Jesse.

---

6. The phrases *As it turned out* and *Just then* in Ruth 2:3–4 suggest moments in time. Mark each phrase in a distinctive way so that you will recognize a change in time or turn in events. How do you explain the timing of these events?

_____

_____

_____

7. What is significant about Ruth's request to both *glean and gather* among the sheaves in Ruth 2:7? Discover further insights below.

_____

_____

_____

Carolyn Curtis James gives us another glimpse into Ruth's request to *glean* and *gather*:

LESSON TWO - DETERMINE YOUR PROVISION

Typically when harvesting a field, hired men went first—grasping handfuls of standing grain stalks with one hand, cutting them off at the base with a sickle, then laying the cut stalks on the ground. Female workers followed, gathering and binding cut grain into bundles to be carted to the threshing floor where raw kernels of grain were separated from the husks. Gleaners came last and were permitted in the field only after both teams of hired workers finished and bundled sheaves of grain were removed from the field.

Ruth requested that Boaz suspend this long-established practice for her. She didn't want to pick up leftover scraps for Naomi. She wanted to feed her mother-in-law. She asked to "glean and gather among the sheaves *behind* the harvesters". (Ruth 2:7, emphasis added) In other words, Ruth asked to go where gleaners were not permitted, to work among the harvesters where plenty of newly cut grain lay waiting to be gathered into bundles.[10]

8. a) List each of the instructions Boaz gives to Ruth in Ruth 2:8–9.

_____

_____

_____

Boaz offers her water whenever she needs a drink. She didn't need to fill a water bottle.

In her book, *The Story of Ruth- Twelve Moments in Every Woman's Life*, Joan Chittister describes the character of Boaz:

> He [Boaz] gives her water out of the buckets drawn by his hired hands in a culture where foreigners were more likely to be slaves than citizens, where women were owned, and where it was women who drew water for men, not men for women.[11]

    b) Describe Ruth's response to Boaz's instructions in Ruth 2:10–13. What does this reveal about her character?

_____

_____

_____

9. a) According to Ruth 2:11, how does Boaz know all that Ruth has done for Naomi?

_____

_____

_____

    b) List three things Boaz notes that Ruth has done since the death of her husband.

LESSON TWO - DETERMINE YOUR PROVISION

_____

_____

_____

    c) What else does Boaz observe about Ruth in Ruth 2:12?

_____

_____

_____

It appears that Ruth gave up everything to follow the Lord, the God of Israel: her father and mother, her homeland, and her people. She gave all these up, even though she had lost her husband who would have been her future provider.

In Genesis 12, we can read about Abraham, who followed God's call in a similar way. Is this not the call of all Christ-followers who have entered into covenant with God through Christ?

Listen to Christ's words in the following two scriptures and then write on the lines provided what Christ is asking of His followers:

LUKE 9:23
Then he said to them all: "Whoever wants to be my disciple must deny themselves and take up their cross daily and follow me."

LUKE 18:29–30
"Truly I tell you," Jesus said to them, "no one who has left home or wife or brothers or sisters or parents or children for the sake of the kingdom of God will fail to receive many times as much in this age, and in the age to come eternal life."

_____

_____

_____

Is it possible to follow Christ in our own strength when He requires our complete surrender of everything? No, it is impossible! We need to be rescued from our fallen nature which seeks only to serve self. All we have to offer God is our brokenness, our past, and all its pain. He offers us a robe of righteousness in exchange for our filthy rags (Isaiah 64:6). His provision has been fulfilled through the sacrificial death, burial, and resurrection of our Lord Jesus Christ.

Although all elements of covenant aren't written in one place together, we can discover different covenant rituals scattered throughout the pages of Scripture. Each element has a significant truth to apply to our spiritual development.

> d) One such element, the exchange of robes, is found in 1 Samuel 18:1–4. Write in your own words what took place as Jonathan made a covenant with David.

LESSON TWO - DETERMINE YOUR PROVISION

1 Samuel 18:1–4

After David had finished talking with Saul, Jonathan became one in spirit with David, and he loved him as himself. From that day Saul kept David with him and did not let him return home to his family. And Jonathan made a covenant with David because he loved him as himself. Jonathan took off the robe he was wearing and gave it to David, along with his tunic, and even his sword, his bow and his belt.

_____

_____

_____

David is symbolically putting on Jonathan. In the New Testament, Galatians 3:26–29 reminds us that we are clothed in Christ. In order to *put on* Christ, we need to *put off* our old self.

> e) Write below what it is that we *put off* and then *put on*, according to Ephesians 4:22–24:

You were taught, with regard to your former way of life, to put off your old self, which is being corrupted by its deceitful desires; to be made new in the attitude of your minds; and to put on the new self, created to be like God in true righteousness and holiness.

_____

WOMAN OF WISDOM

_____

_____

There is such beauty to be found in understanding God's covenant. The imagery of putting on Christ's robe each day helps us to apply these profound and life-changing truths.

This next question reveals another beautiful gem of covenant.

> 10. a) Reread Ruth 1 and 2. Mark every reference to kindness in a distinctive way.

The word kindness in these verses is actually the Hebrew word *hesed*. Scholars have a very difficult time translating it because there is no English equivalent. Some of the meanings from *Strong's Concordance* are kindness, mercy, good deed, favour, beauty, kindly, and lovingkindness. Lovingkindness is a covenant word used in the Old Testament.

> b) Read the following references and underline each mention of lovingkindness. Write on the lines below how God expresses *hesed* to His people.

Psalm 42:8, NASB

The Lord will command His lovingkindness in the daytime; and His song will be with me in the night, a prayer to the God of my life.

LESSON TWO - DETERMINE YOUR PROVISION

Psalm 59:16, NASB
But as for me, I shall sing of Your strength; yes, I shall joyfully sing of Your lovingkindness in the morning, for You have been my stronghold and a refuge in the day of my distress.

Psalm 103:4, NASB
...who redeems your life from the pit, who crowns you with lovingkindness and compassion.

Jeremiah 31:3, NASB
The Lord appeared to him from afar, saying, "I have loved you with an everlasting love; therefore I have drawn you with lovingkindness."

_____

_____

_____

Carolyn Curtis James explains it this way:

> They [Hebrew scholars] tell us *hesed* is a strong Hebrew word that sums up the ideal lifestyle for God's people. It's the way God intended for human beings to live together from the beginning—the "love-your-neighbour-as yourself" brand of living, an active, selfless, sacrificial caring for one another that goes against the grain of our fallen natures.

Two parties are involved—someone in desperate need and a second person who possesses the power and the resources to make a difference. *Hesed* is driven, not by duty or legal obligation, but by bone-deep commitment—a loyal, selfless love that motivates a person to do voluntarily what no one has the right to expect or ask of them. They have the freedom to act or walk away without the slightest injury to their reputation. Yet they willingly pour themselves out for the good of someone else. It's actually the kind of love we find most fully expressed in Jesus. In a nutshell, *hesed* is the gospel lived out.[12]

11. What instructions does Boaz give to his men in Ruth 2:15–16? Based on what we have learned about *hesed*, how is he showing *hesed*?

_____

_____

_____

12. What is the result of Ruth's perseverance in the field in Ruth 2:17? How much was an average gleaning for a day's work? How did Ruth's amount compare to that average?

_____

_____

LESSON TWO - DETERMINE YOUR PROVISION

Ruth was a hard worker, determined to do whatever it took to provide for her mother-in-law and fulfill her covenant promise, made in Ruth 1:16–17.

She boldly asked to glean beyond what the law dictated and gathered far more than an average male worker would glean in a day. Scholars estimate that Ruth had brought home approximately twenty-nine pounds of grain.

13. Read Naomi's comments about Boaz in Ruth 2:20. What name does she give him?

_____

_____

_____

14. Write down all that you know about a kinsman-redeemer. Don't worry if you're just now hearing the word for the first time. We'll cover that topic more fully next lesson.

_____

_____

_____

15. Write below what covenant truths you have observed in Ruth 2.

_____

_____

_____

16. How will you apply these truths to your life this week? Be specific.

_____

_____

_____

Ruth is making some amazing discoveries about God's provision and blessings for those who follow Him in covenant. As we leave Ruth 2, the following excerpt from Arnold Fruchtenbaum summarizes it well:

> Three basic observations can be made concerning Chapter 2. First: Ruth finds *chesed* [*hesed*] in the eyes of Boaz on one level, but on a higher level, also in the eyes of God. Her loyalty to Naomi in Chapter One was now being paid back by both God and man. Second: Naomi and Boaz never meet in this chapter; Ruth has served as an intermediary between Naomi and Boaz. However, if the childlessness of Naomi is to be resolved, it will now obviously involve Ruth. Third: God has begun His

LESSON TWO - DETERMINE YOUR PROVISION

payment of Ruth's wages; the generosity of Boaz was only the down payment.[13]

Lesson Two Summary Statement
"Entering into God's covenant determines your provision."

Memory Verse:

Ruth 2:12

May the Lord repay you for what you have done. May you be richly rewarded by the Lord, the God of Israel, under whose wings you have come to take refuge.

Write out the memory verse on the lines provided.

_____

_____

_____

WOMAN OF WISDOM

Notes

LESSON TWO - DETERMINE YOUR PROVISION

Notes

The Story: Alma, Part Two

You are precious in My sight!

Where had that thought come from? With it fresh in my mind, my hands trembled as I opened my Bible. I had hoped to have a few quiet moments on the flight to catch up on my morning devotions.

Suddenly, I became acutely aware that I was exactly where God wanted me to be. I was taking my two friends to Chattanooga, Tennessee to be trained as Bible Study leaders. They were seated in another section of the plane and I was alone.

Two years earlier, we had moved from Atlanta where I had been involved for a short time with an in-depth Bible study. There my eyes had been opened to new insights in God's Word as I began to learn more about my Creator. How I hated leaving my Atlanta group.

However, waiting for me in my new community were eight women ready to begin an in-depth study, but with no leader to guide them. I agreed to help them temporarily until a qualified leader could be found. *I am not a leader.* Several courses later, our numbers had grown but still no leader had emerged. In a short time my family would be moving again and it was vital to leave a qualified leader in my place.

As I sat with my friends in the training classes for the next week, it slowly began to dawn on me that I, too, had the skills of a leader. That came as a total surprise to me, but that was the beginning of a whole new development in my life. For the next thirty years, wherever I have lived, I have led in-depth Bible studies.

God has promised in Psalm 32:8, *"I will instruct you and teach you in the way which you should go; I will counsel you with my loving eye on you."* How exciting it is to live in this covenant relationship with God, allowing His Spirit within to lead me in the path He has chosen for me.

LESSON TWO - DETERMINE YOUR PROVISION

God used those years of studying His Word to give me a deeper understanding of who He is. He is my place of refuge, my strength, my Rock, my Saviour, my Comfort, my Provider, my covenant-keeping God.

I desperately needed these lessons to prepare me for what lay ahead. In those early days, I couldn't have imagined the trauma that would face me. My thirty-two-year marriage broke up. My family split apart.

My heart is going to break, I thought. *Oh, Lord, God of miracles, restore my marriage.*

Early one morning, the phone rang. My dream of reconciliation ended. My husband had taken his own life.

My covenant-keeping God held me steady. He is faithful in all His promises. He wept with me through the deep valleys, always offering His presence to comfort me and give me fresh hope for the future.

I am precious in His sight.

Lesson Three

Determine Your Family

Dinner conversation in Old Testament culture would have included tales of all the wondrous things God had done for the sons of Israel. Stories like Ruth were passed down orally to each succeeding generation.

Because of their instructions to pass on what they had experienced, the topic of covenant probably made its way to table talk as well.

How wonderful it is to be reminded of God's ways and His promises. This lesson is filled with God's promises and what it means to have a covenant relationship with Him. There are things we can expect from God, and He from us, as we walk in covenant together. It is so exciting!

In Ruth 1:16–17, Ruth made a covenant with Naomi that she would never leave her, that she had accepted Naomi's God, the God of Israel. In Ruth 2, Ruth began to live out her promise to bitter and broken Naomi. Now, as we begin Ruth 3, Naomi begins to respond to

Ruth's kindness, humility, and devotion, and her concern turns to provision for Ruth.

Culturally, men bore the responsibility to look after the women in their families. But where are the men in this story? Dead. Gone. The only characters carrying the story are two broken women—widowed, childless, destitute, with no hope of future economic security, no more sons to care for them or carry on the family name. Widows were viewed as having little value and considered a burden on society. All seemed hopeless.

Ruth and Naomi shared widowhood in a patriarchal culture where being a single woman meant being physically, emotionally, financially, and socially vulnerable.

As we begin this lesson, pause and ask God to show you what truth He wants you to glean this week.

The Study:

1. Read Ruth 3. Jot down your initial thoughts.

   _____

   _____

   _____

The barley was fully harvested. Only the winnowing remained. Although Naomi was still grieving, still had no heir, she lifted her head to see a possibility. It was the right season, the right timing, and she acted!

2. Ruth 3:1 reads, *"One day Ruth's mother-in-law Naomi said to her, 'My daughter, I must*

LESSON THREE - DETERMINE YOUR FAMILY

find a home for you, where you will be well provided for." Can you see any change in Naomi's attitude as we begin Ruth 3?

_____

_____

_____

Author Liz Curtis Higgs writes, "Now it's Naomi's turn to be used by God in Ruth's life. There's something so right about that. A sense of balance and fairness that life doesn't always deliver, but God definitely does."[14]

Finding a home for Ruth had been part of Naomi's prayer of blessing in Ruth 1:8–9:

> Then Naomi said to her two daughters-in-law, "Go back, each of you, to your mother's home. May the Lord show you kindness, as you have shown kindness to your dead husbands and to me. May the Lord grant that each of you will find rest in the home of another husband."

Arnold Fruchtenbaum writes, "Now God was about to use Naomi to answer her own prayer. This is an example of the divine and the human working together to carry out the purpose of God."[15]

3. a) What was the biblical provision for childless widows? Read the verses below

and write in your own words how God made sure the widows were cared for.

Deuteronomy 25:5–6, NASB

When brothers live together and one of them dies and has no son, the wife of the deceased shall not be married outside the family to a strange man. Her husband's brother shall go in to her and take her to himself as wife and perform the duty of a husband's brother to her. It shall be that the firstborn whom she bears shall assume the name of his dead brother, so that his name will not be blotted out from Israel.

_____

_____

_____

b) For whom was this scripture from Deuteronomy written? Would the instructions apply to either Naomi or Ruth? Why or why not?

_____

_____

_____

LESSON THREE - DETERMINE YOUR FAMILY

Deuteronomy was written to sum up and remind the sons of Israel of God's covenant with them as they moved into the land He had promised. Remember that Moses passed on to the people the words God had given him.[16] They included the Ten Commandments and additional instructions for living in community and making sure everyone was cared for.

4. How does Naomi identify Boaz in Ruth 3:2? Underline every reference to *kinsman* or *kinsman-redeemer* in the book of Ruth. Scholars tell us that this concept of kinsman-redeemer is most clearly demonstrated in the book of Ruth. Record below any further insights on Boaz.

_____

_____

_____

Arthur Lewis explains the word redeemer in this way:

> The meaning of "redeemer" is illustrated by the care Boaz undertook for Naomi's household. He accepted the role of the *goel*, the male relative who was responsible for the protection and wellbeing of the two widows. An ancient law, the law of levirate marriage, required that a brother-in-law or other male kinsman of the deceased husband marry a widow who had no son in order to perpetuate

the name of the deceased and provide for the widow. Thus, Boaz, became not only Ruth's "redeemer," but he provided salvation for Naomi as well.[17]

If you would like to pursue further study on the topic of redemption, the following references will give you additional insights:

- Redemption of a nation (Exodus 6:5–6).
- Redemption of a person (Leviticus 25:47–49).
- Redemption of the land (Leviticus 25:23–27).

5. a) List the instructions Naomi gave Ruth in Ruth 3:3–4.

_____

_____

_____

b) Was it culturally appropriate for Naomi to instruct Ruth in this way?

_____

_____

_____

c) How did Ruth respond to Naomi's instruction in Ruth 3:5?

_____

_____

_____

What a statement of submission! *"I will do whatever you say"* (Ruth 3:5), and she went down and did everything her mother-in-law told her to do.

Here we see Ruth following through on her covenant promise from Ruth 1:16–17. Ruth wasn't too proud to be under the authority of her mother-in-law.

What a stark contrast we observe when we look back to Lesson One and hear the words of the sons of Israel in response to Moses when he delivered God's terms of the covenant to them. They also promised to follow all the instructions Moses gave them from God, but in their pride they failed to keep their part of the covenant.

Carolyn Curtis James, in her book *Half the Church*, writes:

> Ruth's purpose is not to find a husband for herself but to rescue Naomi's family from extinction. Instead of waiting for Boaz's instruction, Ruth instructs Boaz. She presents a gutsy marriage proposal to Boaz with all sorts of outrageous strings attached, both for her and for him. Her proposal is tantamount to laying down her own life as a surrogate widow for Naomi (a breathtaking act of faith, given her infertility) and recruiting Boaz to join her in rescuing the family of Elimelech. Here Ruth becomes

the ultimate risk-taker, and Boaz, faced with a staggering demand on his resources will prove to be her match.[18]

6. How does Ruth identify herself to Boaz? What is her request?

_____

_____

_____

Ruth may appear to us today as a brash, seductive woman, but this was a marriage proposal according to the culture and levirate law.

Warren Wiersbe gives us insight into the meaning of spreading one's garment over another:

> To spread one's mantle over a person meant to claim that person for yourself (Ezek. 16:8; 1 Kings 19:19), particularly in marriage. The word translated "skirt" also means "wing". Ruth had come under the wings of Jehovah God (Ruth 2:12) and now she would be under the wings of Boaz, her beloved husband. What a beautiful picture of marriage![19]

Ezekiel 16:8, NASB

"Then I passed by you and saw you, and behold, you were at the time for love; so I spread My skirt over you and covered your nakedness. I also swore to you and entered into a covenant with you so that you became Mine," declares the Lord God.

LESSON THREE - DETERMINE YOUR FAMILY

Carolyn James adds further insight on Ruth 3:9 ("Spread the corner of your garment over me, since you are a guardian-redeemer"):

> Startled awake in the dead of night by the presence of a woman lying at his feet, this man of impeccable integrity discovers once again from Ruth that there is far more to God's law than complying with the letter. Pharisaical tendencies in all of us make the walk of faith doable. We can be moral, go to church, read our Bibles, and give our ten percent. Jesus and Ruth knock down the walls of that kind of thinking. Real kingdom living is costly. It will stretch, bend, and break us. Following Jesus isn't the path to a tame or easy life. It is about taking up a cross—which means laying down our lives as Jesus did for the sake of others.[20]

7. How does Boaz respond to her request?

_____

_____

_____

What an exciting story. As you look at Ruth, do you wonder what compelled her to perform such radical actions? Could it be that Ruth was responding to the call of God on her life, the covenant promise she had made back in Ruth 1?

I remember the day when I knew it was time to leave my job as a sales executive and pursue my calling. I couldn't get away from the promise I had made years before, to do anything God wanted if He would just get me out of my depression. He answered my prayer and it was time to take action.

8. Have you sensed God's call on your life? Take some time to share with each other.

_____

_____

_____

9. Why was Boaz impressed with Ruth's petition?

_____

_____

_____

10. What were his instructions to her? Was it culturally appropriate for her to be at the threshing floor? Explain.

_____

_____

_____

LESSON THREE - DETERMINE YOUR FAMILY

11. In Ruth 3:15, how does Boaz show further kindness (*hesed*) to Ruth?

_____

_____

_____

Not only does the Bible record stories of selfless serving, there are countless people every day who exhibit this scriptural principle. At the end of this lesson, you can enjoy the inspiring story of Henrietta Mears, a woman who gave up a man she loved in order to follow God's call to serve Him.

When we follow the call of God on our lives, we have a new manager, one who cares for us in ways we have never before known. He wants us to serve Him only.

Priscilla Shier, in her Bible study book *Gideon: Your Weakness. God's Strength*, gives us deeper insight into this service to our covenant partner:

> In the ancient Near East, people sealed relationships between individuals or nations by covenant. When larger, powerful nations and smaller, weaker ones made a covenant, the entities operated like father and son or master and servant. Each had a distinct role to perform.
>
> The more powerful kingdom (called the suzerain) would adopt the smaller one (the vassal). In exchange for the vassal's allegiance, the suzerain would provide military protection and financial provision in times of need. The suzerain had authority over the vassal. It might allow the vassal to maintain its own government

and traditions, but it maintained legal ownership of the vassal's land and agricultural harvest.

The vassal was expected to operate in submission to its suzerain. In addition giving a percentage of its annual production, the vassal was expected to be completely loyal. A vassal could only have one suzerain. Making a covenant with another suzerain was high treason and would incur horrendous consequences. The vassal's loyalty was pledged to the suzerain and could not be shared with another.

The Bible translates this kind of loyalty using the Hebrew word *hesed*. It means love, faithfulness, or covenantal faithfulness. A vassal's faithfulness was described as love expressed to his suzerain. Rebellion was to hate the suzerain.

When Yahweh made Israel a nation through Abraham, He used a means people in that era would understand. He cut a covenant. Yahweh became their Suzerain, offering them His unfailing protection and ongoing provision in exchange for the *hesed* of the vassal. They were to have no other suzerains.[21]

12. Note the threads of covenant you have discovered in Ruth 3. Write below how these truths will affect your life this coming week.

_____

_____

_____

LESSON THREE - DETERMINE YOUR FAMILY

Arnold Fruchtenbaum helps us to glean the rich nuggets of the third lesson as he writes:

> Chapter 3, in summary, shows an answered prayer and major developments of the themes in the story. The situation by the end of this chapter is that Naomi's prayer of 1:8–9 is about to be answered: Ruth will find *manaoch* or rest in marriage. The famine will no longer be a factor, since Boaz's gift ensured the women would have plenty to eat. Ruth no longer identifies herself with her lower status, the Moabitess, but with her own name, *I am Ruth;* she was no longer simply just the Moabitess. Theologically, the focus in this chapter is on human activity through the providence of God. God is clearly viewed as the One bringing all these plans and events together, and human *chesed (hesed)* is clearly displayed and is rewarded by divine *chesed (hesed)*. This chapter also further develops the themes of the story regarding the famine, the heir, and Ruth's future. The lack of food comes to an end with the gift of grain; the pair of women will from henceforth be provided for. The provision for an heir for Elimelech has been given new hope. Ruth will yet receive additional wages from God in terms of the provision of marriage. And finally, Ruth has moved closer to being integrated into the commonwealth of Israel.[22]

We are discovering life-altering truths from this book filled with godly wisdom. Ruth discovered it was necessary for her to leave her earthly family to gain an eternal family.

Every principle has its application for today. Our prayer is that you continue on and finish the course. With just one more lesson and chapter to come, we still have many more ways to apply and grow in what we have learned. Wow!

Lesson Three Summary Statement
"Entering into God's covenant determines your family."

Memory Verse:

> Ruth 3:9
> "Who are you?" he asked.
> "I am your servant Ruth," she said. "Spread the corner of your garment over me, since you are a guardian-redeemer of our family."

Write out the memory verse on the lines provided.

_____

_____

_____

_____

_____

LESSON THREE - DETERMINE YOUR FAMILY

Notes

Notes

Lesson Three - Determine Your Family

The Story: Dream Big, Surrender All

I, Ruth, recently read about the life of Henrietta Mears (1890–1963), a remarkable woman who totally surrendered every part of her life, including romance, in obedience to God's will. Her story is told in *Dream Big: The Henrietta Mears Story*, and I hope you enjoy it as much as I did.

Henrietta had fallen in love with a man who wasn't a Christian. She agonized over his proposal, eventually coming up with this thought:

> Marrying this man, fine though he was, would be like establishing a home and deciding that each night the husband would dine in one room and the wife in another. They would both have an excellent meal, but they would have no fellowship together. If, in the matter of their faith, they could not sit together at the same table and have fellowship, their relationship would be an impossible one. Her inner conflict was great, for this was the time of her greatest decision. In the solitude of her room, she prayed: "Lord, you have made me the way I am. I love a home. I love security, I love children and I love him. Yet I feel that marriage under these conditions would draw me away from you. I surrender even this, Lord, and leave it in your hands. Lead me, Lord and strengthen me. You have promised to fulfill all my needs. I trust in you alone."[23]

Truly Henrietta grasped what it meant to be in a covenant relationship with God, and she lived in the reality of what God expects from us and what we can expect from God.

She records:

> The marvellous thing has been that the Lord has always given me a beautiful home; He has given me thousands of children; He has supplied every need in my life, and I've never felt lonely. Since I am a very gregarious person, I thought I would have a feeling I didn't belong. But I never had it, never! I've never missed companionship.[24]

She started off as a teacher in Minnesota and later joined the First Presbyterian Church in Hollywood, California where she became director of Christian Education. The Sunday School grew from four hundred fifty people to four thousand in less than three years, and she developed lively lessons that she later published when she founded Gospel Light, one of the most respected publishers of Sunday School literature today. She is also known for mentoring three young men who later went on to impact their world and reap huge spiritual harvests: Bill Bright, founder of Campus Crusade for Christ; Richard Halverson, a pastor who later became chaplain for the U.S. Senate; and evangelist Billy Graham.

I finished the book inspired and challenged by Henrietta's life. I thought about the millions of lives she had impacted because of her love and commitment to God, and her obedience and unselfish love to see the next generation follow the call of God.

Henrietta knew that her call to single life was her unique call. When young women wanted to be like her and remain unmarried, she was quick to say, "Nonsense! The Lord intends for you to marry; that is the way He has made us. It just so happens that in my case that wasn't His will."[25]

Henrietta points out that God's call is personal to each of us, words of wisdom for today's godly woman.

Lesson Four

DETERMINE YOUR ETERNAL BRIDEGROOM

What does a single decision have to do with your provision or your destiny? Does it really make any difference? Isn't it enough to do the best you can and let everything just fall into place? These are common questions. Perhaps even today, some of you reading this book wonder why you've picked up this study in the first place.

God's plan of redemption for all of us is laid out in Ruth's beautiful narration. Pictures and parables from the Old and New Testaments (Old and New Covenants) are God's way of showing us eternal truth.

Life can become complicated in this twenty-first century, with distractions on every side. By maintaining a singular focus on our God who made us, wants the best for us, and wants to live with us forever, everything else can be simplified.

It's hard to believe that we are already on the last lesson of this study. As you begin today, take an extra moment to be still and recognize the vital part that God has in your story. Then pray that your teacher, the Holy Spirit, will show you a truth that will greatly enhance your spiritual journey. He has a nugget for you.

The Study:

1. Read Ruth 4. Jot down your initial thoughts.

___

___

___

2. a) Mark every reference to *kinsman-redeemer* in the same way that you did in Lesson Three. How many times do these words appear in the book of Ruth: *redeem*, *redemption*, and *redeemer*?

___

___

___

b) Also mark in a distinctive way the words *elders* and *witnesses*. Write on the following lines what you learn about each.

___

LESSON FOUR - DETERMINE YOUR ETERNAL BRIDEGROOM

_____

_____

3. Read the following scriptures to determine the significance of going to the *town gate* (Ruth 4:1). After each scripture, write what transpired at the town gate.

2 Samuel 19:8
So the king got up and took his seat in the gateway. When the men were told, "The king is sitting in the gateway," they all came before him.

_____

_____

_____

Joshua 20:4
When they flee to one of these cities, they are to stand in the entrance of the city gate and state their case before the elders of that city. Then the elders are to admit the fugitive into their city and provide a place to live among them.

_____

_____

_____

4. a) What are the key facts that Boaz presents to the kinsman-redeemer in Ruth 4:3–4?

_____

_____

_____

b) Why does the kinsman-redeemer turn down Boaz's offer? What are your thoughts about his decision?

_____

_____

_____

5. In Ruth 1, we determined that Orpah made a logical decision to return to Moab, based on Naomi's suggestions. Do you see any similarities between this and the kinsman-redeemer's response?

_____

LESSON FOUR - DETERMINE YOUR ETERNAL BRIDEGROOM

_____

_____

JAMES 1:5
If any of you lacks wisdom, you should ask God, who gives generously to all without finding fault, and it will be given to you.

We are free to make any choice we like, but the consequences of our choices, for good or bad, follow naturally. It is important that we ask God for His wisdom in making our decisions.

6. Read Ruth 4:7. Why did the kinsman give his sandal to Boaz?

_____

_____

_____

As Abraham—and many years later, Joshua—walked through the Promised Land, he indicated that they were taking possession of what God had already given them. When Naomi's relative gave his sandal to Boaz, he demonstrated that he was handing over his right to purchase the property. In the future, if Boaz was ever challenged on his legal right to own this land, he would have the sandal as proof of the transaction.

7. a) How would Naomi benefit by having a kinsman-redeemer (Ruth 4:14–15)?

_____

_____

_____

b) Read the following scriptures. Who is our kinsman-redeemer? Write on the lines provided how we benefit from our kinsman-redeemer.

Romans 3:24
...and all are justified freely by his grace through the redemption that came by Christ Jesus.

1 Corinthians 1:30
It is because of him that you are in Christ Jesus, who has become for us wisdom from God—that is, our righteousness, holiness and redemption.

Ephesians 1:7
In him we have redemption through his blood, the forgiveness of sins, in accordance with the riches of God's grace...

Hebrews 9:15
For this reason Christ is the mediator of a new covenant, that those who are called may receive the promised

eternal inheritance—now that he has died as a ransom to set them free from the sins committed under the first covenant.

_____

_____

_____

8. a) What accolades are given to Ruth in Ruth 4:15? In light of her Moabite past, what are your thoughts about such positive praises?

_____

_____

_____

Ruth didn't allow her former life to determine her future destiny. Some of us today have a tendency to focus on our sinful past, either what we have done or what has been done to us.

I, Ruth, can relate, for I felt disqualified from being used by God because of the sins of my youth. I felt the love and call of God as a little girl, wanting only to serve Him. In my longing for love, during my high school days, I naively wandered from the path of purity. I felt ruined, guilty, and useless. Thankfully, as I have become a student of God's Word, I have made a wonderful discovery: I have a redeemer, one who bought me back from my life of slavery to sin. All of scripture is a continual story of redemption.

I talk with women at many conferences, retreats, and Bible studies. Many of them also feel disqualified from God's plan for some sin they have committed or offence that has been done to them. Often they say, "I know God has forgiven me, but I can't forgive myself." Some of you may be able to relate.

To be whole in mind, body, and spirit, each one of us must come to a place where we understand God's forgiveness and redemption, and accept that Christ's blood sacrifice is sufficient to cover every sin. That's why He died.

We all need to follow Ruth's wise choice: she did not allow her past to determine her destiny.

Imagine what a huge portion of scripture would be missing if Saul, later Paul, had allowed his murderous lifestyle and persecution of Christians to keep him from pursuing the task Christ had for his future. When he encountered Christ through the blinding light on the Damascus road, he knew he had been created for something better. He made a conscious choice to focus on what Christ had done for him, and moved on to the prize.

> ### Philippians 3:13–14
> Brothers and sisters, I do not consider myself yet to have taken hold of it. But one thing I do: Forgetting what is behind and straining toward what is ahead, I press on toward the goal to win the prize for which God has called me heavenward in Christ Jesus.

It takes mental discipline and divine help to forget our sins and the sins of others. Perhaps you, like the apostle Paul and many of us, need to move beyond some circumstances of your past.

LESSON FOUR - DETERMINE YOUR ETERNAL BRIDEGROOM

b) Write about your decision to move on from your past.

_____

_____

_____

How differently the book of Ruth would read if Ruth hadn't made a choice to move on and follow Naomi's God. She entered into covenant with the Living God, who is able to redeem what has been lost and transform us into His likeness. Each one of us faces the same choice that Ruth had: to live in our past or turn and go to Bethlehem, the place of Messiah's birth, the house of bread.

9. Write below any new benefits Ruth may have enjoyed because of her strong covenant promise, declared in Ruth 1:16–17.

_____

_____

_____

10. What does the name Obed mean? How is this name significant in light of his future role?

_____

_____

_____

11. Below find the family tree of Ruth. Note the relationship of Naomi and Ruth to Israel's greatest king, David. Note where the new baby, Obed, fits into the family tree.

Ruth: _____

Naomi: _____

LESSON FOUR - DETERMINE YOUR ETERNAL BRIDEGROOM

Ruth's Family Tree

Abraham
Genesis 11:26-31
Matthew 1:2
⬇

Judah
Genesis 29:30-35
Matthew 1:2
⬇

Perez
Ruth 4:18
Matthew 1: 3
⬇

Boaz - **Ruth**
Ruth 4:21   Ruth 4:13
Matthew 1:5   Matthew 1:5

⬇

Obed
Ruth 4:17
Matthew 1:5
⬇

Jesse
Matthew 1:5
⬇

David
Ruth 4:17
Matthew 1:6

Lot
Genesis 11:27
⬇

Moab
Genesis 19:33-37
⬇

⬇

God is faithful to His promises, from Abraham, Isaac, and Jacob on to all those who enter into a covenant with Him

12. Contrast Naomi's circumstances in Ruth 1 and in Ruth 4.

Ruth 1

_____

_____

_____

Ruth 4

_____

_____

_____

As we come to the close of our Ruth study, we want to go back a few pages in the unfolding story to consider one of the most beautiful covenant pictures: that of the wedding.

God initiated the first wedding in Genesis, and finished off Revelation, the last book of the Bible, with the wedding to end all weddings. Jesus performed His first miracle at a wedding and made sure that the guests had the best beverage going, right down to the last drop.

Many covenant rituals are included in weddings, and while we may not recognize them, some of the practices performed in weddings of

LESSON FOUR - DETERMINE YOUR ETERNAL BRIDEGROOM

this century also contain covenant elements that date back to ancient Near East society.

After months of planning, the wedding day arrived. Heather, our beautiful daughter, married Matt Lamarre. Pastor Shawn Spence performed the ceremony as Bob and I watched, misty-eyed.

The vows, the rings, the unity candle, the music and communion all wove an intricate tapestry, each strand adding brilliant colour to this covenant celebration. The delighted couple walked to the registry table, draped in white linen with the bride's Calla lily bouquet cascading over its edge.

With shaking hands, Matt and Heather signed the legal document that recognized them as a married couple. Approaching from either side of the table, the best man and matron of honour added their signatures, indicating their witness to this momentous occasion.

Then, at Heather's and Matt's request, Pastor Shawn called on our senior church leaders, Pastor and Mrs. Don Rogers, and the elders of the church to gather around them. They laid hands on the newlyweds, dedicated them to the Lord, and spoke a blessing over their marriage.

As I recall this emotional day, I marvel at the many elements of their marriage service that drew from God's language of covenant.

13. Which element(s) of covenant described in my daughter's wedding are expressed in Ruth 4:11-12? Write your observations.

_____

_____

_____

Marriage is a covenant agreement between two people made before God.

Genesis 2:24
That is why a man leaves his father and mother and is united to his wife, and they become one flesh.

Although no details are given in scripture regarding the actual marriage ceremony, Steve Herzig lists four of its elements in his book, *Jewish Culture and Customs*.[26]

A. The betrothal period, which lasts a full year.

Deuteronomy 20:7
Has anyone become pledged to a woman and not married her? Let him go home, or he may die in battle and someone else marry her.

B. Singing, beautiful romantic singing.

Song of Solomon 4:1–7
How beautiful you are, my darling! Oh, how beautiful! Your eyes behind your veil are doves. Your hair is like a flock of goats descending from the hills of Gilead. Your teeth are like a flock of sheep just shorn, coming up from the washing. Each has its twin; not one of them is alone. Your lips are like a scarlet ribbon; your mouth is lovely. Your temples behind your veil are like the halves of a pomegranate. Your neck is like the tower of David, built with courses of stone; on it hang a thousand shields, all of them shields of warriors. Your breasts are like two fawns,

like twin fawns of a gazelle that browse among the lilies. Until the day breaks and the shadows flee, I will go to the mountain of myrrh and to the hill of incense. You are altogether beautiful, my darling; there is no flaw in you.

Jeremiah 33:11
... the sounds of joy and gladness, the voices of bride and bridegroom, and the voices of those who bring thank offerings to the house of the Lord, saying, "Give thanks to the Lord Almighty, for the Lord is good; his love endures forever." For I will restore the fortunes of the land as they were before,' says the Lord.

C. One week of feasting.

Genesis 29:22, 26–27
So Laban brought together all the people of the place and gave a feast... Laban replied, "It is not our custom here to give the younger daughter in marriage before the older one. Finish this daughter's bridal week; then we will give you the younger one also, in return for another seven years of work."

D. Consummation of the marriage.

Genesis 29:23, 30
But when evening came, he took his daughter Leah and brought her to Jacob, and Jacob made love to her... Jacob made love to Rachel also, and his love for Rachel was greater than his love for Leah. And he worked for Laban another seven years.

Is there anything more beautiful than a wedding? The light in her eyes, the longing in his, and the anticipation of both, all make for an exciting celebration.

The commitment of a married couple, one to another, may be the only picture some people will ever see of God's love for us. In the New Testament, Jesus is portrayed as our eternal bridegroom. Who is the bride? Those who have responded to His offer of love. Christ's bride is also called the church, or His body. There are so many nuggets of covenant truth in this picture of marriage.

> 14. Read the following verses. The intimacy intended for this relationship with Christ is revealed in these scriptures. Write down any observations you have.

John 15:4–5, 9

Remain in me, as I also remain in you. No branch can bear fruit by itself; it must remain in the vine. Neither can you bear fruit unless you remain in me. I am the vine; you are the branches. If you remain in me and I in you, you will bear much fruit; apart from me you can do nothing… As the Father has loved me, so have I loved you. Now remain in my love.

_____

_____

_____

15. In light of all we have learned about marriage and its covenant significance, write down your observations. Include any other signs or symbols you might observe at a present-day wedding.

_____

_____

_____

And now, the wedding to end all weddings!

REVELATION 19:6–9

Then I heard what sounded like a great multitude, like the roar of rushing waters and like loud peals of thunder, shouting: "Hallelujah! For our Lord God Almighty reigns. Let us rejoice and be glad and give him glory! For the wedding of the Lamb has come, and his bride has made herself ready. Fine linen, bright and clean, was given her to wear." (Fine linen stands for the righteous acts of God's holy people.)

Then the angel said to me, "Write this: Blessed are those who are invited to the wedding supper of the Lamb!" And he added, "These are the true words of God."

Note that, in the Bible, fine linen represents the righteous acts of the saints.

When I, Ruth, married my husband Bob over fifty years ago, he and I pledged our love and faithfulness one to another. Because of this pledge of commitment (entering into covenant), I gained something unique that day, something intangible but life-changing. I received a new name. Since that time, I've been entitled to many benefits that I would otherwise not enjoy. To use the name Coghill legally, I must be married to a Coghill—in my case, Robert W.

    16. a)   In our marriage to Christ, what name do we acquire?

REVELATION 2:17
Whoever has ears, let them hear what the Spirit says to the churches. To the one who is victorious, I will give some of the hidden manna. I will also give that person a white stone with a new name written on it, known only to the one who receives it.

_____

_____

_____

        b)   What privileges do we have because of our covenant commitment to Christ?

JOHN 17:11
I will remain in the world no longer, but they are still in the world, and I am coming to you. Holy Father, protect them by the power of your name, the name you gave me, so that they may be one as we are one.

LESSON FOUR - DETERMINE YOUR ETERNAL BRIDEGROOM

Colossians 3:17
And whatever you do, whether in word or deed, do it all in the name of the Lord Jesus, giving thanks to God the Father through him.

_____

_____

_____

17. Write in your own words how this study, *Woman of Wisdom*, has helped you to see God's plan for all eternity.

_____

_____

_____

The longer I live, the more I've come to understand how quickly this life passes, just a speck of time in light of eternity. When you and I accept Christ's invitation to be married forever, it is truly a 'happily ever after' story. I've accepted the invite, have you?

18. Now that you have gleaned a few elements of covenant, how will you live with these principles in mind? Be specific.

_____

_____

_____

Lesson Four Summary Statement
"Entering into God's covenant provides your eternal bridegroom."

It all started in Ruth 1 with a journey to Bethlehem. Each succeeding chapter indicated another reason to go to Bethlehem, the house of bread, where Jesus, the Bread of Life, started His earthly existence. There is so much more to learn as we focus on Him and His birthplace.

- Lesson One: Entering into God's covenant determines your future.
- Lesson Two: Entering into God's covenant determines your provision.
- Lesson Three: Entering into God's covenant determines your family.
- Lesson Four: Entering into God's covenant provides your eternal bridegroom.

LESSON FOUR - DETERMINE YOUR ETERNAL BRIDEGROOM

Memory Verse:

Ruth 4:14
The women said to Naomi: "Praise be to the Lord, who this day has not left you without a guardian-redeemer. May he become famous throughout Israel!

Write out the memory verse on the lines provided.

_____

_____

_____

_____

_____

_____

Notes

LESSON FOUR - DETERMINE YOUR ETERNAL BRIDEGROOM

Notes

The Story: The Mystery of the Bride

Our Lesson Four story features the writing of Jonathon Cahn in *The Book of Mysteries* and highlights the deep relationship we have with Jesus when we enter into the eternal covenant. Enjoy the truths expressed in this wedding narrative.

> On our journey to the city, we stopped on a nearby hill.
>
> "Look," said the teacher, pointing to an event at the city's edge.
>
> "It looks like a wedding," I replied, "or the preparation for a wedding." The bride, in a white gown, was standing in a garden with her bridesmaids.
>
> "You're watching a cosmic mystery, the shadow of a mystery. Existence," he said, "is a love story… or was meant to be a love story. The bride is a picture of what we were each created to be."
>
> "I don't understand."
>
> "We were created to be the bride. That's why we can never be complete in ourselves. That's why, deep down, in the centre of our being, in the deepest part of our heart, we seek to be filled. For the bride is made to be married. So we can never find our completion until we are joined to Him who is beyond us. And that is why we go through our lives trying to join ourselves…"
>
> "Join ourselves to what?"
>
> "To that which we think will fill the longing of our hearts—to people, success, possessions, achievements, money, comfort, acceptance, beauty, romance, family, power, a movement, a goal, and any multitude

of things. For the bride was created to be married, and she can never rest until she is."

"So none of the other things can work?"

"No. None of the other things are the Bridegroom."

"And who is the Bridegroom?"

"The Bridegroom is God, the One for whom we were created."

"So we have to find Him."

"More than that," he said. "A bride doesn't just find the Bridegroom; she *marries* Him. So it's not enough to find God; you must *marry Him.*"

"Marry God? How?"

"By joining every part of your life and being—your deepest parts, your heart, your soul, your wounds, your longings, your desires, everything—to God. Only then can you be complete. Only then can your deepest needs and longings be fulfilled. For the mystery of our hearts is the mystery of the bride. And the bride can only find her completion in the Bridegroom. And the Bridegroom of our souls…is God."[27]

Appendix:

Extra Story and Wisdom Verses

The charm and beauty of the book is well illustrated in an incident involving Benjamin Franklin, the American Statesman and inventor. When serving at the French court he heard some of the aristocrats "putting down" the Bible as being unworthy of reading, lacking in style and so forth. Though not personally a believer himself, his youth in the colonies had exposed him to the excellence of the Bible as literature. So he decided to play a little trick on the French. He wrote out Ruth longhand, *changing all the proper names to French names.* Then he read his manuscript to the assembled elite of France. They all exclaimed on the elegance and simplicity of style of this touching story.

"*Charmant!* But where did you find this gem of literature, Monsieur Franklin?"

"It comes from that Book you so despise," he answered—"*la sainte Bible!*"

There were some red faces in Paris that night, just as there should be in our own biblically illiterate culture today for neglecting God's Word."[28]

Each of the four lessons in this study, *Woman of Wisdom*, includes a verse to memorize from the corresponding chapter of Ruth. The four verses provide a scriptural summary of key principles of covenant. Why not write out the four verses on Notes page 88,89?

We pray that you'll be encouraged now to commit to memory a few of the wisdom scriptures printed below. Then you'll have an instant resource hidden in your heart to help you in your daily walk.

Wisdom Verses:

Job 28:28
And he said to the human race, "The fear of the Lord—that is wisdom, and to shun evil is understanding."

Proverbs 9:10
The fear of the Lord is the beginning of wisdom, and knowledge of the Holy One is understanding.

Proverbs 9:12
If you are wise, your wisdom will reward you; if you are a mocker, you alone will suffer.

Proverbs 1:7
The fear of the Lord is the beginning of knowledge, but fools despise wisdom and discipline.

Proverbs 3:19
By wisdom the Lord laid the earth's foundations, by understanding he set the heavens in place.

Psalm 90:12
Teach us to number our days, that we may gain a heart of wisdom.

Matthew 11:25
At that time Jesus said, "I praise you, Father, Lord of heaven and earth, because you have hidden these things from the wise and learned, and revealed them to little children."

Matthew 12:42
The Queen of the South will rise at the judgment with this generation and condemn it; for she came from the ends of the earth to listen to Solomon's wisdom, and now something greater than Solomon is here.

1 Corinthians 1:19
For it is written: "I will destroy the wisdom of the wise; the intelligence of the intelligent I will frustrate."

1 Corinthians 1:25
For the foolishness of God is wiser than human wisdom, and the weakness of God is stronger than human strength.

1 Corinthians 1:30

It is because of him that you are in Christ Jesus, who has become for us wisdom from God—that is, our righteousness, holiness and redemption.

1 Corinthians 2:4–5

My message and my preaching were not with wise and persuasive words, but with a demonstration of the Spirit's power, so that your faith might not rest on human wisdom, but on God's power.

Colossians 1:9

For this reason, since the day we heard about you, we have not stopped praying for you. We continually ask God to fill you with the knowledge of his will through all the wisdom and understanding…

James 1:5

If any of you lacks wisdom, you should ask God, who gives generously to all without finding fault, and it will be given to you.

James 3:13

Who is wise and understanding among you? Let them show it by their good life, by deeds done in the humility that comes from wisdom.

Wow! You have completed the third book in the WOW series. We hope that you have enjoyed this study as much as we have enjoyed preparing each lesson. God's Word is so powerful. Each time we look at a passage, it is as though something new emerges, fresh and appropriate for this time in our lives.

We pray that you will continue to explore the life-changing topic expressed in covenant, the language of God, as we have only skimmed the surface.

Watch for the fourth book in the series, *Woman of Worship*, which will lead you into a study from the Old Testament tabernacle, set up by Moses in the wilderness, to the New Testament fulfillment of that which was foreshadowed by each article. More life-changing truth from God's Word!

The four books in the series are:

- Woman of Worth: Lifelong Encouragement From Psalm 139
- Woman of The Word: A Memorizing Scripture Experience
- Woman of Wisdom: Threads of Covenant Woven through the Pages of Ruth
- Woman of Worship: Entering God's Presence, from the Old Tabernacle to the New

Until we meet again, know that God's plan is always the best and His Word will never fail.

Isaiah 40:8
The grass withers and the flowers fall, but the word of our God endures forever.

Contact Information

ruth@wordstoinspire.ca
www.wordstoinspire.ca

Endnotes

Introduction

1. Arthur Kay, *Our Covenant God: Learning to Trust Him* (Colorado Springs, CO: WaterBrook Press, 1999), 49–50.

Lesson One

2. Note that Chemosh, the detestable idol of Moab, required human sacrifices. See Numbers 25:1–4.
3. We'll cover this topic further in Lesson Four.
4. Sinclair B. Ferguson, *Faithful God: An Exposition of the Book of Ruth* (Bridgen, UK: Bryntirion, 2005), 20–21.
5. See Covenant: A Brief Overview in this book's introduction.
6. Each of the four lessons will have a summary statement that emphasizes a deep truth.

7. *Woman of the Word: A Memorizing Scripture Experience*, the second book in the WOW series, provides a step-by-step process to memorize Psalm 8 and to make the spiritual discipline of memorizing part of your daily routine. Imagine learning a passage of scripture with other women, each one responsible for a verse or two, and then at the end of a month reciting together the entire psalm! *Woman of the Word* is filled with stories of people whose lives and circumstances have changed because of God's Word hidden in their hearts. *Woman of the Word* and other valuable resources are available on our website: www.wordstoinspire.ca.

Lesson Two

8. Arnold G. Fruchtenbaum, *Ariel's Bible Commentary: The Books of Judges and Ruth* (San Antontio, TX: Ariel Ministries, 2007), 307.
9. Ibid., 305–306.
10. Carolyn Curtis James, *The Gospel of Ruth: Loving God Enough to Break the Rules* (Grand Rapids, MI: Zondervan, 2008), 101.
11. Joan D. Chittister, *The Story of Ruth: Twelve Moments in Every Woman's Life* (Grand Rapids, MI: Eerdmans, 2000), 49.
12. James, *Gospel of Ruth*, 115.
13. Fruchtenbaum, *Books of Judges and Ruth*, 317.

Lesson Three

14. Liz Curtis Higgs, *The Girl's Still Got It* (Colorado Springs, CO: WaterBrook Press, 2012), 106.
15. Fruchtenbaum, *Books of Judges and Ruth*, 319.
16. See Lesson One.
17. Arthur Lewis, *Judges/Ruth* (Chicago, IL: Moody Bible Institute, 1979), 108–109.

ENDNOTES

18. Carolyn Curtis James, *Half the Church* (Grand Rapids, MI: Zondervan, 2011), 92.
19. Warren Wiersbe, *Be Committed: An Old Testament Study of Ruth and Esther* (Colorado Springs, CO: David C. Cook, 2008), 53.
20. Curtis, *Half the Church*, 93.
21. Priscilla Shirer, *Gideon: Your Weakness. God's Strength* (Nashville, TN: Lifeway Press, 2013), 15.
22. Fruchtenbaum, *Books of Judges and Ruth*, 336.
23. Earl O. Roe, ed., *Dream Big: The Henrietta Mears Story* (Ventura, CA: Regal Books, 1990), 81.
24. Ibid., 82.
25. Ibid.

Lesson Four

26. Steve Herzig, *Jewish Culture and Customs* (Bellmawr, NJ: The Friends of Israel Gospel Ministry, 1997), 54.
27. Jonathan Cahn, *The Book of Mysteries* (Lake Mary, FL: Frontline Charisma Media, 2016), 6.

Appendix

28. William MacDonald, *Believer's Bible Commentary* (Nashville, TN: Thomas Nelson, 1995), 287–288.

Coming Soon:

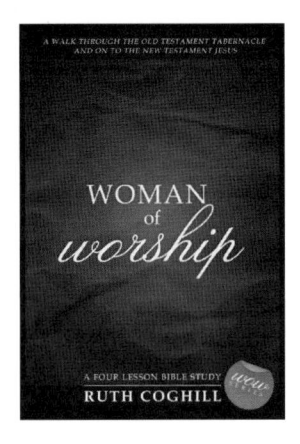

WOMAN of worship
A WALK THROUGH THE OLD TESTAMENT TABERNACLE AND ON TO THE NEW TESTAMENT JESUS
A FOUR LESSON BIBLE STUDY
RUTH COGHILL

Also Available:

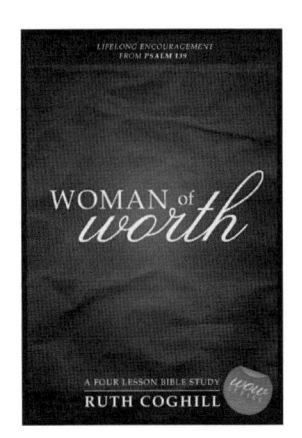

Woman of Worth paperback!

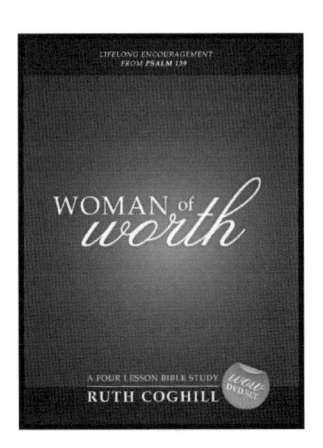

Woman of Worth DVD!

Woman of the Word paperback!

For more information and to purchase product go to:
www.wordstoinspire.ca

To contact Ruth:
ruth@wordstoinspire.ca